# EXILES
## Among You

# EXILES
## Among You

# KRISTJANA GUNNARS

COTEAU BOOKS

Edited by Geoffrey Ursell.
Cover painting by Kate Scoones, "Red Canyon."
Cover design by NEXT Communications.
Book design and typesetting by Ruth Linka.
Printed and bound in Canada.

The publisher gratefully acknowledges the financial assistance of the Saskatchewan Arts Board, the Canada Council, the Department of Canadian Heritage, and the City of Regina Arts Commission.

Poems from this collection have appeared in *Event, Poetry Canada, Arc, Matrix* and *Dandelion*.

**Canadian Cataloguing in Publication Data**

Gunnars, Kristjana, 1948-
        Exiles among you

Poems.
ISBN 1-55050-093-7

      I. Title.

PS8563.U574E95 1996   C811'.54   C95-920940-9
PR9199.3.G793E95 1996

COTEAU BOOKS
401 - 2206 Dewdney Ave.
Regina, SK Canada
S4R 1H3

*Dedicated to the memory of Tove Christensen,*
*my mother*

*"I am the raven-mother; I am the raven-mother," each raven croaked, and Anne Lisbeth felt that the name also applied to her; and she fancied she should be transformed into a black bird, and have to cry as they cried....*

🍂 Hans Christian Andersen, "Anne Lisbeth"

beloved: for that is your name
the name that will be after the blue mountains
this word is all I can give you: gifts
unheard of as ghosts wander paths
that are highways for refugees

I speak to you all this time from the dark
moss-grown hemlock woods
baby squirrels mastermind the foliage
debris of former years on the ground

cedars fallen over from exhaustion
because to live, to live exhausts them
their roots split up from the soil in walls

those giants crash among trembling ferns
and grass-shaped mushrooms with beady heads
when I walk here the old growth tree trunks
crumble under my feet: once tall
I can see the earth carries on with its multitudes

## ❧ 2 ❧

many days I have kept silent at the sea
where posts jut out wrapped in wire
to barricade some boat that never comes

the low lying hills seem tired
overgrown in green fatigue and the sky
too leaden for this time of year

even the salt water seems brown
and sailboats for some reason absent
their captains transfixed at the sight of waves

as they search the gravel banks, this place
envelopes the unspoken years in me
this pier holds on to what is not there

a barnacle covered bridge
grown old in its ocean
starfish glued to the posts
and grass: grass perched on the tops
of old logs in crazy defiance
big rusty nails that hold the lot
in its absurd conjunctions

I have come here again to see
things fall apart, slowly
hoping the small riplets that eat
our bridge where it meets water
will teach me what the river
taught the ferryman
in Siddhartha's own torn robe

❦ 4 ❦

it is so hard to see the sun
stunned behind trees
in this thick forest: a canopy
of branches nets the sky

through the ceiling of leaves I see
how the sun gleams
too starkly for the human eye

I am told not to look directly
such grandeur can only be seen aslant
the way you see a poem: love

I have a river
it is a clear river, it rustles along
over stones and small boulders in its bed
it is a river of shadows
when the sun soaks through the trees
the water is embraced by shade
here and there across its body
arms and fingers and thighs stretch
and elsewhere outcropping rocks
are hot with sun
the crowns of trees hang like willows
as if they were curtains of a room

I am frequently here
at the banks of my river
I like to put my hand in the water
both hands in the cool stream
I can see all reflections there
the green shadow, the white sunlight
seem to say it was never wrong
to keep your memory fast as a stone
and let the flow of my thoughts
wash over

it was not you in my thoughts so much
as the thought of you
and as I tell you this a small boat
sails straight towards me, lights blaring
white on top, a red on one side
green on the other: do we come or go
my nautical charts are not here
which way to turn; the procedure at sea

so much like life on land
as the northern sky flares up in sunset
with the stain of sweet wine
I can tell them I was drunk with thought

and why do they say it is not a fairy tale
world? have we not been kissed
by the glacier, and awoken again
by the daughters of the sunbeam? like this

foxglove madness just outside my door?
they careen out of the ground each spring
a purple and white profusion of bells
jangles from tall stalks in all directions
and in each foxglove flower is a face

just like a vision of the goblin in the cellar
who came up every night to look at the student
reading under the face tree
the tree with faces hanging on every branch

as days pass, one after one
I become used to sunset
spreading over the water, a body
lit from within, used
to receding mountains, fading
every dusk into pastel shadows

used to the space that defines me
to myself, photographs in frames
wooden statues on a ledge, half
burnt candles in candelabras
an open book on the library stand
mugs on a mugrack, wine glasses
upside down on the butcher block

strange to say I am home
with this auburn sky, russet water
I become used to peace

every time the old man cuts wood
with his axe, the silence breaks
sharp interruptions chop
a place in my mind, split
every time the axe falls

someone saws, someone hammers
sound carries in the country
in nature's silence, each
movement turns monstrous

but I wait, the sprinkler
many acres away, the bobcat
many forest miles to the north
in my ear, through
the ringing and pounding

for I imagine in the end
which is not an end but beginning
you will stand there, unexpected
and instead of the low-flying sea plane
it will be you I hear, your voice

## 10*

because there are so many ways of saying a thing
he says he falters
each word poised
as for a great leap, luxurious
breathtaking, daring finality

because I have written this, now
I can die, he says
my book my last testament
my will: the last word

because a writer is secretly content
a fathomless abyss to fall through
the writer pares himself on cliffs
of absolution, lunges
into the depths of a lifetime

the surging currents below:
every word jumping into the unknown

*Conversation with V.S. Naipaul.*

## 11*

because we came out of the ice
crocuses unbuttoning spring
snow geese returning earthward
we are caught on the tips of grass fingers

held there in contemplation
wherever we move the earth moves with us
abject in tiger lily kerns
they say we were here, rounding
out the silver spheres of moon and stars
in coats of diamond studded ice

in green agony of ice
and numb forgivings of dawn
but we are here, palm fronds waving
in equatorial breezes, at last
waving as if to say good bye to the north

*The migrations of the Icelanders.

# ◆ 12*◆

how did we build all this heartache
out of fractured vapour, drops
indiscernible to the eye
out of fractions of seconds
how we broke time like communal wine

until our days lay scattered, innumerable
decimals of what we did not live
we, magicians of the avalanche
wherever we stepped the ground turned
to dust, to ashes, how we raised
such clouds of crying:

what you thought was rain, those
are the children floating there
all the children, paying for us
with bodies they never asked to have

*Civil war in Rwanda, 1994.

take this last little sunshine
that was here yesterday, yesterday
was word perfect

all the towboats are in harbour
doilying about like little black ants
on the kitchen counter: where
did they come from, those little
spoilsports: out of nothing

such a tiny tug pulling an ocean
liner like that out to sea

pulling the sunshine in me
out over the mountains: happy day
that gave me impeccable speech

I hope you have the force of angels
guarding the remnants of summer
I no longer have: sailing
on the heavy sea like that
out of earshot

*il pleut*
*pleuvait, plut, pleuvra, pleuvait*
*qu'il pleuve:* it rains in my sad thoughts

the sand on the beach is wet
stalks of driftwood persist after
tumbling on waves for God
knows how long, they restfully soak

sometimes I wander here alone
and catch the cold storm on my collar
my hand is not as small as it was

the boats here bob, floats
on fishing lines are suspended
on the surface of an unsettled sea
small knobs of memory hang there

as heavy rain tries to puncture
holes in the skin of ocean
I sometimes wrap my raincoat

a little tighter to my chest
and tell myself little French verbs

I woke up from the dream of my mother
born for the last time when she died

who was she? that dreamer herself
in her rocking chair by the back window
with her violets and cacti on the sill

the older she became, the dreamier
her eyes clouded over in a mist of longing
her face turned upwards, always to the sky

I did not know she was so given to prayer
I did not think her wings were so untouched
how she dipped their tips in the pools of tears

she must have been shedding in her silence
I did not know there was this silence in her

I could tell she left us long before she died
passed into a heaven of her own
and our final good byes spoken long, long ago

places that held me, once
their wings enclosed: buttercups
on a windy plateau, saxifrage
in a damp meadow. the marsh I stepped in

engulfed me, its soggy momentum
outcropping my canvas shoes
ducks there, mergansers and geese
not knowing the world was larger
and pigeons, and swans in a line

such small enclosures we took
to be all: places
that have embraced me before
when I struggled from their grip

still call with the moaning of doves
and crying of ravens and the hot breath
of arctic terns, wings adrift, screeching
screeching: exile, come home

## ❧ 17 ❧

mother, I have stood on a crowded street
waiting for pennies to fall
for taxis to stop, for doors to revolve
like this: and I have thought it was you
long after you died: you there

shopping for a diamond, bending to make
straight the edge of your dress, raising
your head and laughing, laughing again

is it unreasonable? in this nameless city
to see your face in all those other faces
approaching in a crowd, so many of you
your one face become a hundred
on any given day, that I have seen you
over and over, like a film projected
gone awry, like a film in which you star?

everything I asked for became
mine, so much so
I was afraid of asking

thinking there are angels
not flying, not swooping on wings
but angels that walk the night

the way the caller of hours did
in the ancient city, one who walked
the winding streets, chanting

matins, vespers, midnight
the closing of the gates
and these angels give: if you speak

with the mouth of prayer, the heart
beating an unconscious rhythm

because some are touched
by the wings of a blue butterfly, lost
in the hemisphere, a green calipash
motion come to rest on your arm

as if pointing to you: come
between the nest and the sky
between the mist of the sea and heaven

a wing so graceful the oaks curl
with their mandarin roots: take
the pallor from the lips of the water
waken the cowrie shells from sleep

and you did, I know you did
the shadow of lost wings in your eye
praying there, makes you careful
the gentle transformations in your hand

because you move with the steps of folded
wings, I can tell

on the day Tenzin Gyatso, the fourteenth
Dalai Lama of Tibet, rode
across the Himalayas, a child of a man
into India, out of the Asian
Land of Snows, in a numbing blizzard

I was a smaller child in the European
Land of Snows. on that day
I packed a canvas bag full of dried fish
a linen hat and rubber boots, left
my father's house: destined to cross
the great lava fields

I heard my father call my name
turning in the street, backpack hanging
I saw him in the doorway of our house
"where are you going?" he asked, gentle
the way feathers fall off the kitiwakes

who is to say? which direction is north
or east or where we need to go
when we leave home, or what tidal currents
lodged in the oceans of eternity
pull us out into the breaking seas

the sand on the beach is not smooth
but clings to the beach towel
to the goosebumps on arms, to toes
cooled with the chill of ocean

that fluid body, separating
what is light, can be washed ashore
the debris of shattered dreams
leaving all our heavy days to sink

so I quietly pick up my sullen limbs
and emerge from the resounding waves
the way beings have always walked up
to put on the weight of time

to exist inside this illusion
to batter fury against the glass
of light, to hum inside our golden cage
signals of distress to the sun

when I think of you I can only think
of the many times we have said good bye
so many partings I wonder how the world
holds together when so much comes apart

and how hardened the arteries of experience
become, how immobile the impossible sorrow
that we have gone from the parting of lovers
a hurried kiss in a railway station

the lingering of arms in arms in airports
when the universe seemed toppling around us
and carts and baggage and people running
made the moment distill itself like the eye

of a tornado, to the insecure holding of hands
in a busy thoroughfare, caught in the sunlight
when we did not know in what manner to greet
each other or how to say our farewells

like strangers with a dim memory of past lives
I send you off now feeling as old as the trees
as though I were the elder, grown wise with you
and watch you go with a numb ache in my heart

if you thought it was a simple thing
to see dust flying in the air of silence
cowling on the roadside, armed beggars
in an incongruous world, think again

I know you do not believe the blasting
transformers along the road
how they burst at every new flash
the lightning of our intentions

think again. a movement of the head
can be as silent as the bleeding
fuchsias hanging on their stalks
and as sharp as word of mouth

your mouth: my mouth. if it could be
so simple, I would let dust fly
let the dust fly where it will
and settle in the folds of time

# 24*

at least there will be a day
of mourning, flags half-way
slashing the wind where earth meets sky

at least the penstemons will be dead
on the roadside, the irises gone
all that flowering broom, over

and at the very least a day of rest
when the fanfare is finished
and the courtyard emptied

I have discovered so many deaths
undergone in the course of living:
the death of rain, of summer, of desire

and death has so many agents
even as you walk into the fall pagoda
hair blowing, placing your hand

and there is a blooming flotilla
crowds of people waving tiny flags
because we thought you would return

it was such a public love
but in the end, curtains drawn
only I know why I cry

*Kristján Eldjárn, third President of the Republic of Iceland, died
unexpectedly on September 14, 1982.

in the dungeon of our language, we
could meet, still
as the cast iron press stands
unused on leaden legs, little
letters filed for words on the block

in the dampness of the words
we could breathe, musty scaffolds
and cobwebbed bottles lined
little brigades of delirium
we could reach out our arms and swim

always hoping for an eternity
of meaning in our clothes
on our tongues, our hands
the cryptograms of the heart
palm on palm, some day to see
that killer whale surface at last

in the night, darkness raging
I unfolded a batten lace tablecloth
from the Republic of China, white
cotton, and ironed it in the kitchen
six napkins with lace corners
and I spread them on the mahogany table

glass crystal candelabras, four
sterling silver wine goblets on a tray
I lit an ornamental Victorian lamp
as if expecting night company

now I know how those women felt
whose men were fishing the Grand Banks
and the others whose men were in trenches
or in jungles wearing camouflage
and the widows, I know them too
the ones who continue to expect the dead
the crazy ones, the mad ones in the attic

I count thirteen years today
since I was with you on the ice
since we sailed among floes
the glass sea engulfing us
in the ice palace of our home

you said we were exiles even then
roaming like a lost cake of ice

I have stood with those days, those weeks
and years in my hand
what do I do with this glass cupola
that has become a toy in the hands of foreigners
they shake it and watch the flakes flurry

you and I inside
forever frozen in place

## ➤ 28*➤

a boy in skin boots
looks out where cranes fly
broad wings in slant motion

a boy packed in cotton quilt
in silk cap, September haze
touches his forehead, warnings

he does not know yet, worlds
engulfed and emptied, he is alone
in an immensity he cannot see

he is all boys, he is
the heir of cold winter
snow on the sides of houses

frost laced water at his lips
he is the boy from Chengdu
whose fingertips touch

soon snow will fall, soon
leaden skies will form, soon
the cranes will have flown

the folds of time on his shoulder
soon he will become tall
and who knows what his mother knows

*In 1992, the government of the People's Republic of China warned
the populace they were raising an army of seventy million males by
refusing to have girl children.*

because the thought of you begins
the thought of endings
I camouflage necessity
speak of primordial dreams

the language of oyster beds
soft liquid in concrete shells
defies endurance

I want no more radio waves
tunnels of light or washouts
of poisoned shorelines

I am alone with my thoughts
direct them to where crows fly
tell them to sweep across

the waters of my memory
spaces so dark no light escapes

what you never see will never awaken
a memory, but sleep there

diluted in milk clouds of spring
a sheath against summer sun

when even forests are earthen grey
and mourning doves linger inexplicably

even the wind slows down, branches
batter less forcefully, ravens

meander as if lost across the air
forget corpses left beside waters

and I am among the alders
horizons closed beyond the bay

I see nothing but granite day
and life itself seems short

wherever waters are calm
places where lips of ocean
speak quietude or rest
sea urchins gather in crowds
starfish untangle
let go their hold of the rocks

in those waters of tranquility
salmon, trout, sea bass, oyster
swim, pebbles lie on shore

sea horses of the imagination
float breathlessly in the deep
the canoe glides over
soundless on the blank surface
a poem in wood
that lets the current navigate

directionless it floats
my own thoughts without anchor

and if a small drop falls
exactly off the edge of the drainpipe
with momentary elegance
the way it ran down a rusty roof

the aluminum pail fills
since so much expertise overflows
the cold steel I call home
chills at the touch of rain

then the ocean weighs down
whatever it discards
such as a halibut carcass
inexplicably found on shore

the same exactitude I expect
in a microchip, computer
manifested wisdom, so exact
the smallest  tundra lily

alone in a misty heath
trembles at the breeze
a drop glows against light
and quickly dies

*On May 30, 1994, it was announced the United States and Russia
no longer aimed their nuclear missiles at each other, but had
redirected them to the North Atlantic instead, in the approximate
location of Iceland.

a silhouette in Davis Bay
the ocean silken with milk
the sky satined: a single rowboat
one man in rainhat, one
fishing pole in the air

so often I have come this way
there have been gulls
on posts protruding out of water
a bridge extending nowhere
except to gaze into mist

and today the lone fisher
who like an ancient mariner
appears unexpected, a colourless
shadow afloat all day
who mysteriously disappears
and when villagers ask who?
no one can say: not one

**34***

if I see you in the garden surrounded
by delphiniums and rhododendrons in the shade
serene and unsuspecting, if I pass by
in my broken sandals, how do I greet you?
because I could not speak for you
when you asked, I have hidden in the leaves

to stare at your beautiful shadow
the composure of your whisper and sad
demeanor of your eyes. the stillness around you

my prayers are silent as the grave
my thoughts are locked in the safe of my body
and I can feel the afternoon breeze on my skin

what I cannot even say to you:
that in my sorrow I want to walk on the grass
so slowly, so calmly, so tranquil this moment
and lift my hand to your face in the arbor
and say it was you I loved all along

*On May 30, 1994, Pope John Paul issued a Papal letter declaring
women may never be ordained as priests in the Catholic Church.

on the day of South Africa's first
all-race elections, the alders
are in such bloom, the air full
with new rain, the ocean
always in imitation of the sky
is pale aquamarine. patterns
of current and calm show up
marked by streaks of slow boats
as if writing our stories on blue slate
red breasted robins stand transfixed
and stare at me: newcomer
they squeal and spider web strings
are brilliantly visible when the breeze
blows down the woodside. below
the throated howl of a hooded
owl in the dark. the world
has its languages and I
find myself in the western sun
so far away: I cannot get
those lineups to vote out of my mind:
the desire to have voice. the sounding
difference. the wind in the pines
high above my chair, my pen
my paper: patterns of shaking and stillness
show up. that I came from the world's
oldest democracy*: that I think of
the world's youngest. the perfume
in the spring air is so strong
I carry it in my clothes, hair, so
rich the wind cannot blow it away

*The Republic of Iceland, founded in 874 A.D.

it rains on the surface of the sea
a wind I cannot feel raises
the hackles of the ocean
the lonely paddle I dip down
continues to return, a funnel
inside its wake. there is no sound
not even the patter of drops
or trysting of ripples. all around
the water that once again looks black
as tar, breathes from inside
I can see the chest of the deep
heave and exhale. in the silver
confines of evening I feel sad
with the inlet in my arms, water
rushing between my fingers, I cannot tell
why our caressing is so sad

because I know you are in the hands
of the spectre that gave us birth
the belly of the mountain
where we crawled once in our dreams

you are in the electric air
thin and caustic, air that breathes
north winds of summer, drought
of another year yet to be

when it is dry, when soil cracks
like paper cakes under your feet
when whistling tunnels trap themselves
in your lungs: when the earth turns

I think it will be too late then
and I will have followed the stream
to a western sea, where it opens
into the arms of another mother

it will be I who am gone and be
you left on the dry slopes
where avalanches and avalanches run
while my small hands forever in the sea

until it is you, the hour
of old-growth wood delays
opening into summer green
field berries, salal, hemlock
a forest tied into itself

the door opened swallows
birdsong over every step
wren, pigeon, raven, jay
a host of them, visitors
visitors like me: birds

quail along the road
babies just hatched snap
into the trail where squirrels run
into bushes, into ferns
and popping cedars, old growth

none of this, none of it
lets in the sunshine now
or the glimmer of moon at night
because it is not you
yet, not you, not anything

let me be certain as the sea
that rocks beneath my feet, a slow
boat opts into a teething bay
and mussel shells float everywhere

ahead branches swagger, an evening
sun glowers into mouths of leaves
on distant rainsides trees
scull into taming tomorrow
and flat fish slacken the depths

peaceful as morning meadows, wild
and fragrant with spring
noisy chatterbeaks
strike out again their old old tunes
and I would like to be so sure

touch me your never ending
fingertips of cloud and sky
tell in my ear the gales are in
and the rain, rain hammers my roof

as it did yesterday and the day
before: forever beating out
the drumsong of cities in the chest
the region of pounding

drums that are heard up shore
and also across the strait
even this carries over
and I hear you speaking everywhere

and I gave you my best years
like so many others, so much of me
has gone into the grave with you

the fire burning in my hearth
providential, the flowers blooming
in my windowsill, the sun falling in

through the pane, warming
cold and frosty hours enduring winter
in a bundle of smiles: all

this went into the grave with you
buried now, forever
extinct. and I am resurrecting

myself. I am pulling up
roots of you in my heart
tearing out what is left of you there

**42\***

today I am up before the sun
because rain breaks my sleep
raccoons are in the heavy ferns
one presses a nose against the glass
a bear walks through the yard
pushes over a trash can. I am up
before the thousand birds that rise
to sing dawn into the air
and out of moss-covered hemlock
from under filaments of branches
there are voices inside me
that cry like abandoned infants
beside the sutured stumps

*\*In 1993, the logged stump of the oldest tree in Canada was discovered in British Columbia. The tree was 1,800 years old.*

at this hour everything seems sane
I forgive myself my misdemeanors, forgive
myself having loved you irrationally
at this hour nothing is irrational

the world has a human hue at four a.m.
the angels have not departed for the sky
yet, I can tell they languish
in the bay and have forgotten the time

when the first flush of starlings swoop
over the cedars, robins pipe up
incomprehensible warnings about daylight
and break the spell of night

to think I could be so generous all day
and bless myself with the wisdom of priests
that I did not know what I did: but I did
and to love you with this small breath

of a small atmosphere churning over
hawking wind patterns, air currents
bewildering the sky in their turnings
the large gifts, the gifts of morning

should we not have said to one another
crows dance in pairs of three
hawks have been seen in grottos

even eagles have their days:
should we not have noticed, another
curtain falls across our vision
grey, mud, alabaster sheets

we see them drop from the sky
a region of large predator birds
clouds us in feathers of steam

in this milky obfusion, we
cannot see one another, not
even from the vantage of broad wings

## ❧ 45 ❧

today I have been considering endings
all day, endings so final
that to return to yesterday would be
impossible as blood running backwards

to go back: just poison
that would make all air go out of my lungs
I know it can never be done: yet
thinking of endings is like not thinking
or placing a word in the mind
so unrecognizable, the mind itself balks
and yesterday wells up again, again

in its marigold sweetness, the taste
of honey on my tongue, the smell
of lilacs in my veins, the sight
of the deep eyes of the past in my eyes

so I go nowhere
in one place I listen to rain drop
onto the roof all day
leaves rattle on crooked chains
blasting to be free
even mourning doves, full
in bushes that bend to their weight
even they are gone

a summer tornado, I can tell
from the way the ocean crumbles
leaves skyrocket, tree trunks
crack and the sky falls
and I am safe in this one place
this lotus leaf I call home

afterwards, nothing
afterwards there is a stain of red cherries
a mitre of peacock

tensed so high the air zithers
musical humming crowds into small spaces

the number of cherries never diminishes
there is a memory of baking sun
the highway is steeled with moving cars

and grandstanding pedestrians
as if it were any sunny morning you like
but it is not

this is afterwards

to begin again, after forests
have curved themselves, arbutus
limbs have extended too far
over the cove, breaking
and cloud reamlets dispersed
after too much rain, drained

it is a life of beginnings
whenever new days
arrive, a small boat
floats across the water silent
as if sneaking away from the old

heavy rainwater left to dry
on garden chairs, tables
gleaming puddles mixed in dew
to dry them off, to look out
and see wildflowers open
pink, blue, crimson to the salt air

## ❧ 49 ❧

funny how the raven flies
flagging itself overhead
arbitrating mid-morning haze
how even I care less and less

no flagships on the blue sea
truly the sea is blue today
not even a sailboat in spite of wind
choppy waves, currents awash

how it all goes up in smoke
where there is no fire
just a pink light before noon
signalling an average day

did I think you had entered my days
and then my nights: intruder
you have stooped over my big bed
with the wrought iron railings

I have heard you breathe there
heard your movements in the flurry
of mourning doves crowding a tree
surprised by a door slamming

how they all fly off at once
heavy, like dark velvet-covered spies
at my window, wings trailing
it was you: I know it was you

that it is not a dream, this
bowl of crimson strawberries, glass
of Champagne, this new sun
preening itself on all the leaves
the green dominion around
stroked by breezes: the amours
of morning, renditions
of some long forgotten opera

and it is not a stage, this
veranda with wrought iron
chairs, this table that holds
blueberries off bushes below
and a cedar railing that stands
around us like a guard of honor
not a drama someone wrote
or singers practiced for

just us, you and me, breakfast
over the open sea, white
curtained sailboats glide out
soundless under ivory wings of gulls
and we hold stems of glasses
to touch lips, touch mornings
a beautiful story set to the screams
of warblers on branches

## ◆ 52*◆

the way a cobweb carries the morning dew

drops of water from the air
we can call tears if we want

the eyes are empty now
the blue air is starless
the moon pale

we need a new vocabulary for this

*1994 saw a conflagration of wars around the world, and with them
previously unimagined cruelties.*

we did not recognize each other
I encountered you on a path at night
the way I imagine Tagore surprised his god
after so long

all we can do is shake hands
and gesture kisses we cannot give
I left you with all my words unsaid
and went home to the falling stars

because it was the night of the meteors
I leaned back in a chair on the deck
in a blackness only the country night knows
and there: there: there: the fiery globes

I waited for flew across
against the stationary stars
my meteor collided helplessly
such a long journey: so without end

*Between July 16 and 22, 1994, twenty-two fragments of the comet
Shoemaker-Levy 9 collided with the planet Jupiter.*

a searing sun cuts
the morning haze, before eight
already tiny finches fill
the thousand alder trees

I am without thought so early
in the heat, blank as the day
is new. a bluebird
smashes itself against the window

mirror to the sky. I leave it
lying dazed on the deck, heart
pounding, three hours, four
hours. the tragedies of summer

the heartbeat of this earth
we live on. the mistakes
we make. we all make

dark rain in the city, mist
a block away shrouds buildings
till they are suggestions of themselves

a line of parked cars both
sides of the one-way avenue
Chevrolets all, and Fords
as if by previous design: stage
set for a windy script

street lanterns with curlicues
and cast-iron fencing around
tiny courtyards out front
red brick buildings from the war

a man lives here: he breathes
the rain-soaked air, walks home
at six after the subway
briefcase hanging from the hand

he still wears a hat, the way
it was done in the forties
he looks down every step
shielding his face from the rain

the packed city, full up
and everyone indoors, the street
lonely in its paved self

and I the only one left looking
at the corner in my shoes
beside a dark fire hydrant, a sign
at the curb, the night chill

the green and yellow dead body
of a small finch lies
on the deck. a sunny morning
calm and unbeguiled. bodies
of flies on the floor and bees
weightless by now on the sill
after what must be hours
of looking for escape

this morning after being gone
for a week in the city
I mop up this wildlife
that has battered my house
I returned resolving to love
you no more: now I find
how these small miracles fall
down in my absence

I throw the bird into the bushes
below, the bees and flies
over the ground. in
the kitchen a spider wove
a web across the room
I break it first thing
heading for a cup of coffee

we sit on top of the lifeboats
myself and workers sailing home
Peninsula people: Vancouver receding
behind us in the hot sun
like an unpleasant dream we are waking
out of in a sweat

they laugh: they always laugh
on the way home. there is beer
at home, chairs to put feet up on
and sailing boats in the marina
gulls and mergansers and children
in the waters of the bay

I listen to their energetic chatter
like the gulls, screaming up
shouting across the decks: hey!
close my eyes and feel the evening
sun bathe my arms, legs, face

as we leave port, a wide-
winged bird ascends from its post
like an old, sullen man, grey
blue in the late day
and lands on a cliff to watch us
sail away. I whisper to it

heron, my clandestine prayer

because I have not forgotten
you, my attempts to throw
the memory of you out, as I put
plastic bottles into paper bags
for recycling, the paper bags
themselves for recycling
it all comes back to me

in another form, but back
the way all materials come around
in what they used to call
a vicious cycle: now you are
seated beside me, now walking
in a path in a park, tall
trees providing cover

because we need cover, because
sometimes it rains, rains
memories I have tried to put
away the way people make compost
and allow all things to return
to earth: the way water itself
comes down and returns to earth

# 59*

there is a man looking at his desk
there is a woman at a typewriter
there are others smoking cigarettes
leaning on chair backs, unmoved
and young boys holding walking sticks
and young girls in hats

where the valleys fill with haze
as if a forest fire far away
gave off its breath, entranced, tired
flames invisible, white smoke standing
in columns out of the high hills
an ethereal whisper, someone said what
should not have been said, just now

*Poem for PEN.

I did not think I would find myself
sitting in an empty flat, back
against a bare wall, balcony door
slid open to an evening breeze
above prairie again. did not think
I would come this way again

to be blown about on the shifting
winds this way, to fly in the face
of myself. to retread broken paths
just this once, as if life itself
were eternal, like a sun that never
sets, so far north. as if I had time
to go over lost tracks like this
again, again. so I lean against this

white wall, the first cup of tea
I have in this flat on the floor
next to me, clashing sounds of trucks
in the alley below, screams of children
from the compound next door, the growl
of an airplane straight ahead

so I go slowly through the day
treading on eggshells, shards
of steel, breathing fibreglass
dust: that way, as if danger
were my companion today

as if, as if, not knowing
what is, this once, asking
the blue of the cobalt water
the ochre of the green sky
what they are: what I see

if the lens of my eye records
this filament world, its frailty
not quite conceptualized, only
felt, the way a puff of wind
feels when I lean into the sun

as the weather changes,  unusual
noises in the house wake up
the morning. a window seems
to crack. a corner crimps

from some condensation of cold
or expands in growing warmth
the heat of summer, as the sun
sparks into the forest, ignites

those of us too small to tell
what invisible currents collude
around us. what unheard voices
speak to us of the coming day

that time should be so heavy
Sunday in its leaden coat, mops
up the debris of a week flaunted
the way wedding rice is thrown
into the thin air of disbelief

where did the days go? such
an easy question, spoken in the hum
of evening flies, lost crows
haggling to each other about dusk
I listen in on their argument

where I rest on the veranda
rocking in a chair as though I too
were a hundred years old, nothing
quite so unbelievable as this evening
so out of form, so dark, so askew

how every day we say good bye
to parts of our lives: we see
summer draw to a close the way
curtains are slowly pulled together
and days are shorter, darker, until
total darkness sets in: we see

purple foxgloves that bloomed
at the roadside fall apart until
they are weeds like other weeds
straggly, brittle straw in fall winds
and fireweed, before so pink
now melted away

how we know a season is over
and we must be older, the daylight
deeper, more experience
to draw on, further disappointments
and wisdom in the aftermath: a bundle
we pack on our backs as we go

and why should the corrugations
of my thoughts not make me afraid
for they are not thoughts but reactions
ruffled nerves like the sea at noon
when the wind picks up and you scurry
for shelter in your frail canoe

that in this case you appear unexpected
a wind from the south or north
we cannot tell the direction of waves
or which way trees falter in a storm
they seem to fall and bend in every way

because I am afraid of the disorder
frail wildflowers crumbling in rain
liquid wrecking-balls in the afternoon
you find the yellow and red poppies
squashed against the sandy ground

I tell myself all is illusion
human affairs a cloud in the breeze
you see it cover the sun, then disappear
formations never repeated: never
mist you can walk right through

the only thing real is the sea
satin blank in the dawn
the orange ocean warm and cold
lifts itself and lowers itself in turn
as the earth moves, as the moon travels

the only reality is that I breathe
and my heart pounds, miraculously
every day the same, I wake from sleep
and there is the white sea again
and the white sky in the north
and the thousand year old cedars overhead

I have wandered in these woods
because of the conversations
between eagles: I hear them above

in the tops of fir trees
the melodious chimes they make
surprises me, I never heard
creatures like that, so unmoved
so out-of-reach

they tell me it was not him
I loved but the distance
he placed between him and me

I have wandered these mountain
paths where forget-
me-not flowers crowd
and hemlocks stay green

and  wonder how they knew

a purple violet on my desk listens
to the hum of my electric typewriter
acting out a rhythm from my hands
the language of the body. it hears

from the way the table stirs
when letters are picked, alphabet
of emotions barely encountered
and let go the way caged birds

are freed in some gesture of kindness
letters of absolution. the violet
knows no other life, thinks
human beings are bodies with fingers

that pluck at keys that click softly
letting out a train of feelings
till they are mist in the air

they have lined up for hundreds of years
and crowded in small enclosures

the ones called wretched, the ones
you did not see when you walked by

under concrete bridges, past doorways
the homeless making a bed for the night

the ones who keep arriving after doors
are closed, after lights go off

still there, the ones with no hours
no morning, the people of no time

bees on summer rounds
honey, honey they call

from stalls in a market
a sign that says melons

cucumbers, tomatoes
any day like this will do

wheels that crunch dry
summer dirt, a basket

on my arm, wasted
grass, footsteps everywhere

the haze I took to be cloud
is not cloud, just distance
an unclear thought I had

your eyes are the eyes of ravens

they tell no story
your mouth is that of silent swans

someday all our thoughts will be written
in the pages of morning mist

then we will know
we will be clear as the new rain

the waitress brings lemonade to our
table, under a sagging umbrella
we are sheltered against the sun, the patio
noisy with people we do not hear

we have brought ourselves to this place
to tally up the intervening years
you lean back in the frail chair, calm
I lean forward, surprised

I say you can erase fiction, but
you cannot erase life: undo what once
took place. that you were ablaze
with imagination then, and now you woke up

*"Oh what I would not give to reach my child!" said the weeping mother; and as she still continued to weep, her eyes fell into the depths of the lake, and became two costly pearls.*

🖈 Hans Christian Andersen, "The Story of a Mother"

Kristjana Gunnars is a Professor of Creative Writing at the University of Alberta in Edmonton. She is the author of six books of poetry, two short story collections, two novels and a work of non-fiction, which was nominated for a Governor General's Award. Her essays, stories and poems have also appeared in numerous journals, magazines and anthologies in Canada, the United States and Europe. Translations of her work have appeared in Icelandic, Spanish, Danish and French.

Born in Iceland, Gunnars moved to Canada in 1969 and has studied in Oregon, Saskatchewan, and Manitoba. She has worked in a café in Squamish, BC, imported Danish wooden shoes in Vancouver, and taught school in rural Iceland. Gunnars has taught English at the University of Regina and Okanagan College in Kelowna, BC.

In addition to her own writing, Gunnars has edited a collection of short stories by Icelandic Canadians, a collection of scholarly essays on Margaret Laurence, a book of brief Icelandic folktales in translation, and co-edited a publication of modern Icelandic writing.

Gunnars divides her time between Edmonton and the Sunshine Coast of British Columbia.